We Are Light

Poetry to Shine With

We Are Light

Poetry to Shine With

Copyright © 2023 by Cheryl Lunar Wind

Cheryl's poetry in this collection may be shared, printed with credit given to the author. All other contributors keep rights to their work.

Any Inquiries contact:

cheryl.hiller@yahoo.com

Some of the poems in this collection first appeared in

Know Your Way, Love Your Light, We Are One, Follow the

White Rabbit, and Life: Shared thru Poetry chapbooks;

and on facebook.

Cover credit, photo taken by Rita Chambers, 2023.

Cover design by Catherine Preus, 2023.

First edition.

Published by Sacred Path Poetry, Weed, California 96094

ISBN 979-8-9892496-0-2

Preface

About this collection--

Some may wonder why I create these collections;
going around asking others to contribute their thoughts,
expressions and perspectives through the means of poetry.

It brings me joy to see, hear and feel through others' sharing.
That sharing is a beautiful gift, which I respectfully wrap in
the form of a little book, and then I get the joy of sharing that
gift with all I can.

It's not about owning or competing, more about working together,
encouraging and collaborating. Seeing the beauty in others.
Together--
we are whole.

"Grandmother is with me always--
not the one I have a picture of in my living room---
the eternal grandmother--ancestral--without race or creed.
She holds light in one hand, a staff in the other---feathers
adorn her hair, robe and staff--showing me the way to peace."
---Cheryl Lunar Wind

Where do Bad Rainbows go?
Prism--
It's a light sentence, and gives them
time to reflect.---Unknown Author

Dedicated
to
Gloria Winitz Endres

The Only News I Know

The only news I know
Is bulletins all day
From Immortality.

The only shows I see
Tomorrow and Today,
Perchance Eternity.

The only One I meet
Is God,--the only street,
Existence; this traversed

If other news there be,
Or admirabler show---
I'll tell it to you.

Emily Dickinson

Contents

Light (I have come home) by Cheryl 1

Keep Living by Cheryl 2

We Are Supported by Christine O'Brien 3

A Choice by Maria Lodes 4

(W)hole by Cheryl 5

Linen and Lace by Christine O'Brien 6

The Redesigned Life by Christine O'Brien 7

Rain by A'Marie B. Thomas-Brown 8

Being With Grief by Rajni Lerman 9

Choice by Cody Ray Richardson 10

You Have Options by Susan Grace 11

Messages by Cheryl 12

Choice by Cheryl 13

Poem Slices by Mercy Talley 14, 15

Evolving Self by Maria Lodes 16

The Truth Is... by Maria Lodes 17

A Pleiadian Passing By by Dave Harvey 18

I Am by Dave Harvey 19

Secret Garden by Cheryl 20, 21, 22

Birds by Uncle Chester 23

We Are the Temples of Our Creator's Love 24
by Eileen Casey and Steve Keating

The City and others by Cheryl 25

Explorations by Cheryl 26

Excavations by Cheryl 27

The One Lesson by Cody Ray Richardson 28

Pure Path of Freedom by Cheryl 29

Free Will vs Ownership 30, 31
by Cheryl

Not My Kuleana by Cheryl 32

Birth of Light 33
By Rita Chambers and John Raifsnider

In the Shadows We Met 34, 35
by Jennifer H.

Contributors page

Author page

Light (I have come home)
by Cheryl

I walk in the light---I Am the light.

I shine my light for all to see.

I join the light of my family.

I ride the Rainbow Bridge to my home.

My home is bright---

My father is the Sun.

I have been 'born' on the Mother.

She is returning to the Light.

We are all Light.

I see light, guiding my way home
I feel light, the essence of my soul
I Am light, in my heart I know
that we are light, together we are whole.---Sam Garrett

Keep Living *
by Cheryl

Be the light at the end of the tunnel.

Use your magic for good.

Be thankful for what you got.

You are an alchemist--
take a situation,
transmute it into
something
Better.

Own your gifts.
See clearly,
that you are gifted.

Ride the roller coaster.
Join the dance.
Be the conductor.

Play that funky music--
Shake your tail
Sail your boat
Spread your wings
Enter the art--
Gape. Vibe. Jive.

Name that tune.
Know your way.
Love your life.
Be the light!

* title inspired by A'Marie B. Thomas-Brown

We Are Supported
by Christine O'Brien

With each footfall

upon yielding earth
I am supported.

With the rushing river
its non-clinging ways
I am supported.

In the scattered warmth
of winter's sun
the crystallized heart
learns how to melt.

With the trees punctuating vaporous skies
while delving deepest depths
there is support.

In the llama's aloof stare
the cat's scraping claws
the yearning for a loyal lover
I am supported.

In the exchange of a smile
or kindness
in the midst of the longest,
darkest night
the illusion of our separateness
parts.

Reflected in the retina of
your deep-seeing heart
is the daring dream of unity.
We are supported.

A Choice
by Maria Lodes

In Spaciousness
        there is a choice---
Put aside our suffering
        connect with the Whole...

(W)hole by Cheryl

A black hole is complete---
empty and full---at the same time.

Whole.

Black contains all colors,
rays and energies.

Like a black hole,
the eternal rainbow.
We are complete,
together we are whole.

Linen and Lace
by Christine O'Brien

I discover who I am
as I go.
Thank you for this unfolding
a flower opening out,
petal after patient petal
wanting to be,
waiting to be,
while being.

Not a finalized,
completed essay
of my life.
Nor even a poem that
rhymes me into
wholeness.
Verses strung together,
sometimes,
often,
unwieldy,
obscure,
lacking cohesion,
part and parcel of
an unknown,
unforeseen becoming
yet never arriving.

Content with that,
can I be?
I'll wear linen and lace
as I pass through
gate after gate,
barefoot or
wearing soft soled
white moccasins.
They seem gentle
on the earth.

The Redesigned Life
by Christine O'Brien

Glitter sparkles on a paper peony
as an abandoned Robin perches
on the leafless Cecile Brunner.
The grids of one's life, like vintage obsolescence.
I comb my thinning hair daily
pondering if who I am makes a difference.
Hidden chords are being played;
the native in me listens deeply.
Holding my breath as the lost bee walks
on a tightrope-like icicle--
such fragile beauty is necessary to one's health.
Balance--everyone is talking about it.
What wisdom sits unused?
Which goblet is yet to be sipped?
I am fertile with inspiration this winter.
Swirls of lilac, splats of blue,
the road unfolds up ahead
as I watch the northern migration...
I wonder if we've lost our way.
Beyond the lonely winter are flowery meadows
and puffy clouds, like cats, ready to pounce on solemnity.
Did you realize that your life can be entirely redesigned
by glitter sparkling on a paper peony?

Rain by A'Marie B. Thomas-Brown

Sing in the rain
Breathe in the rain
Run in the rain
Walk in the rain
Shout in the rain
Dance in the rain
Laugh in the rain
Cry in the rain

Supple supplications of sanctity
Dancing on the precipice of peace
Cultivated through persevering through every
Opportunity
That presents itself in our life stream
To converge with our soul purposed destiny
As we create the beauty in living
Connected to the source that is giving
The rain
The sun
The moon
The stars
No holds barred
Naked abandonment
Surrender's dance
Suffering's accompaniment
Balance in hand
So we breathe

Pitter patter goes the rain
Stutter utter is the game
We speak in the rain
Again and again and again

Being With Grief
by Rajni Lerman
www.gaiaservices.net/

Lying in the dark of pre-dawn I feel the grief quietly rumbling there
Somewhere between the heart center
and the belly
A deep ache sits
Unattended, ignored, bulled over by a dozen tools
Tools that seem essential not to fall back into the same human habits again and again, that keep us small, safe, stuck.
They have a place
And I want to hold on to the raw discomfort,
Not run away.
To experience the truth of this moment.
Life is messy, confusing, terrifying
And beautiful, wild, amazing
How do I hold onto the outbreath, that pause, and befriend that dull aching pain?
I acknowledge and feel you.
You are welcome for "you are a part of me that I do not know yet".*

*Valerie Kaur

Choice by Cody Ray Richardson

The truest of all questions is
Can I disperse the mist
Of the illusion that some people cast
Do I know the right questions to ask
Or will my own denial blind my way
Will I get caught in the games they play
Another tool in their box
One more shiny thing they gather like rocks
Will I wake in their dream
What they see could be a nightmare for me
Will I drag them into mine
Or will we build the same design
Play in a world of both our building
Roll in our paradise and act silly
Surf the tide of the rhythm we created
Do simple things the way we stated
The choice is mine to discern
What can we do but live and learn

You Have Options
by Susan Grace

Some things aren't going to change
How you want them to right this hot minute,
If at all.

You can keep gripping and insisting,
But it's just not budging.

Why?

Because misalignment.
Because impatience.
Because timing.
Because you ain't ready for that thing yet.

Keep circling back to you.
Where is your centeredness?
How do you hold peaceful presence?
What is your commitment to taking care
of yourself?
Are you aligned energetically with your want?

You have options.

~ ~ ~

Major life changes don't happen
In one broad stroke.

They happen in the moment,
One choice at a time.

Those choices add up and
You find yourself on a completely different
trajectory.

Possibilities are on offer.
You have options.

Avoid the sameness trap.
Choose differently.

Messages by Cheryl

Dark, night sounds find me,
Resting.

The ceiling fan, speeding along...
No where to go----
Always so insistent.

Finished Matrix 3 earlier.
Message received---CHOICE.
Been a theme lately.

The ringing in my head,
brings a peaceful knowing.
I am on the right path.

The Fortune Teller---
"I know because I must know.
It is my purpose. It's the reason I'm here,
the same reason we are all here."

Lemurian cards came in the mail today.
Message received---
You express your divine will through sound,
words, tones and melodies.

There will be harmony
between
Your humanity and your divinity.

Look up----to the sky.
Cosmic rays, orbs, sunbows, rainbows,
They are the divine delivery personnel.
Message received---Be at peace.

Choice by Cheryl

Kindness is the border I won't cross.
It is the land I reside in.

Fairness is the foliage---

the trees are strength
they are my family.

I Am a walking tree.
Daughter of Solaris,
Child of Gaia.

Gaia has a new gig,
She will be called the Freedom Wisdom Star.

The old way is done.

Our light will shine the way.

The New Earth, 5D--not 5G--

Join Us--->

Light, Color, Music, Sound...

Vibrations are the bridge---

The Rainbow Bridge.

The codes are in the air, you can feel the change.

Sometimes it's hard to breathe,
All the nonsense; the duality, the tension...
What will we be?

It Is a Choice.

Poem Slices by Mercy Talley

There is
Deep Healing
In this Moment With
The Tender Touch Of Love

~ ~ ~

How Deeply
I Let Go
Is How Profoundly
I'll Remember
How Whole
I Am

~ ~ ~

My poems are
Peaceful Prayers
I breathe upon
the wings
Of Doves
To Seed
The Bird Tribes
With Remembrance

~ ~ ~

Poem Slices by Mercy Talley

All
Distortions
Are
Grinding
To A Halt...
Time To Stop &
Reconnect
With Clarity
To What Is True
Distraction Free

~ ~ ~

To the nuclei
of deception
This Ray of Light
Pierces with
Truth
Potent & Pure
Love Victorious

~ ~ ~

Evolving Self
by Maria Lodes

Given free will
   ---become who I Am
Evolving self
   ---god's holy experiment

Pretending qualities
   ---godlike in nature
My imagination
    begins to take off---

Embellishing a persona
   ---adorned with pride
I project myself
   an endowed being...

Having practiced so long
   being god---
What must it be like
   <u>*Being*</u> *God...*

The Truth Is...
by Maria Lodes

The Truth of misery
    lies in deception---
A broken heart
    seeking love outside---

The Truth of anguish
    hides in deception---
Wounded pride
    seeking perfection---

The Truth Is
    ---Realizing who I Am
There is no suffering
    only love...

A Pleiadian Passing By
by Dave Harvey (2022)

Feel to heal
A smile is hope
Create your own luck
Look for the new growth
Be patient in your rebirth
A recipe for peace dear one
---A Pleiadian passing by.

I Am
by Dave Harvey (2023)

I am accepting the mystery in front of me
I am imagining the best possible outcome
I am feeling for every opportunity to love
I am forgiving my shortcomings
I am allowing my whirlwind of emotions
I am manifesting freedom
I am dreaming of ecstasy
I am studying compassion
I am loving the beauty of nature, of you, of all
I am unafraid of the chaos
I am basking in my potential
I am crying for the abandoned
I am laughing with the carefree
I am running with the wolves
I am flying with the owl
I am becoming what I've always been
I am bowing to the divine in you.

Secret Garden by Cheryl

In Oz,
Dorothy
was looking for a way back home---

A spell, talisman, or the wizard.
What did she learn
on her journey?

The wizard could not
give her
what she already had.

Don't Forget
the ancient magic---
We all carry.

You take your wand
where ever you go.

We each have
a Secret Garden---

There,
You can
Access your hidden magic.

Hear the elemental song.

Meet with fairies and pixies.
Sit in circle with Sasquatch.
Listen to the flowers.

The shine of a sparkling creek---
carries the wisdom of the ages.

Our guides
> direct our path
> and protect us along our way.

In my garden
> the Unicorns stand guard---
> only the pure of heart may enter.

We all have a guardian angel---
Fairy
Unicorn
Dragon
Crystal
Tree or
Crow,
as unique as we are.

Like the fireflies
they offer light---
Serve as guideposts along the way.

Dorothy
went on a journey
to learn about magic.
Find her way home.

By helping others
she found her way.

This path
Elusive
Can not be forced.
Can not be captured, bottled or sold.
You can find it---
In the wisdom of the owl
Fire of a dragon
Flight of a fairy
And from the strength of unicorns.

They say---
"It's not the destination, but the journey."

This one rings true.

At any time
We feel lost
We can visit
our own
Secret Garden---
where we have many helpers.

They are patient
guiding us
Until
we Remember
our power---

and find our way home
like Dorothy did.

Birds by Uncle Chester, NightWalker
June 3, 1943- August 24, 2023

Birds, birds--in the sky,
look how beautiful--they do fly,
they fly and fly, those beautiful birds in the sky

Although there are many kinds
they must have very humble minds
for they never seem
to quarrel or fight.

Even tho there are many kinds,
sometimes they seem to say
why can't you be as gay?

Some day we'll be just as gay--
In God's new world
to sing and play.
To my knowledge, I think--
that this is not so far away.
Then we'll hear those birds
and understand their beautiful words.

We Are the Temples of Our Creator's Love
by Eileen Casey and Steve Keating

I listen to the sound of Holy Spirit as I walk upon the Earth.
Birthing my true brilliance I know of my hearts worth.
I Am Soul and I Am free to be expressed as who I Am.
Sharing my Soul gifts with all of life.
I know that I can.

I can do anything I can imagine.* I can do everything that I can dream.
I Am a sacred temple of Divine love and I can do anything my heart believes.

I surrender to my karmic lessons and the light comes pouring through.
I stop, ask, and know just what I need to do.
I sing songs with gratitude such as the Holy Hu.
Give thanks for life's blessings and the gift of loving you and I can do anything I can imagine.
I can do everything that I can dream.

I Am a sacred temple of Divine love and I can do anything
my heart believes.

We are the temples of our creator's love and we can do anything our hearts believe.

*I wish to give thanks to my beloved Steve Keating for the inspiration of the sentence "I can do anything I can imagine" after I shared what I had previously written. I am grateful and blessed for the gift of knowing and loving you.

The City by Cheryl

Rain drops
like bombs.

Doves soar,
above the city,
rising high.

Give up the half of it--
Daily grind.
Keep up. Win. Compete.
Rappers trill on and on--
wear bling and
eat fried fingers--
flaming fondue.

Beach Scape by Cheryl

Flamingos--
pink umbrellas--
nature's architecture.

Mamba by Cheryl

She was a prim dame,
wore a vest of Yeti Yarn--
Walked with a cane,
its duck head recited the Raven.

The Sad Man by Cheryl

The sad sayer walks around,
wearing a scarf like a turban.
Speaking, Leaking sad words,
Inviting you to join him.

Explorations by Cheryl

Exploring a cave at dusk---
I found a lute, in a dirt lair.

I ran all the way home
to make curfew--

By my window
I played my new instrument.

Listening,
a star took flight--
Became a Dragon--
landed on my roof.
Thud.

The neighbor's dogs
yipping
excitedly.

Excavations by Cheryl

What gifts do you have buried?

Go in that cave--
deep down, clean it out.

The deeper you dive
the higher you'll fly.

Come fly with me---
fold time and space.

Dive into the sun--
Go there,
this now moment--
Fly free.

The One Lesson
by Cody Ray Richardson

Letting go---
truly
clearly move on.

It's all a role.

---One Lesson---
      to learn how
      to let go.

"Don't try to hold on to anything."
"What we never had."

"Grow with it, then let it go."

If we are to make it out,
we must let go.

Pure Path of Freedom
by Cheryl

Freedom is Walking the Pure Path.

Wearing your true colors---

Freedom is being yourself
Following your own drumbeat,
                        dream,
                            truth.

Take the Pure Path of Freedom.

"If you wish for your path to be a sacred one,
then act like a Sacred One."---Chief Golden Light Eagle

Free Will vs Ownership
by Cheryl

In the language I was raised with, English---
things are described as in relation to belonging.

This, that----yours, mine.

Very young children are taught---
rights of ownership.
"Mine"

Relationships--
familial and romantic are described this way--
my children, my husband, my partner
My, My, My

Society demands payment for necessities;
such as homes, cars, food, clothes--

Is it any wonder, with receipt in hand,
we say---
my car, my snack, my apartment, my room?

Pets--
my cat, my dog.
Ownership.

My space, my time--leave me alone.

The prophet Gibran states--
'we do not own our children,
they are like arrows shooting
out to space'.

Is this why we are here? to collect
and own as much as possible?

Birds, trees and the earth
give their gifts freely--

Feathers, eggs, leaves, nuts, wood,
rocks, sand, water, ponds, creeks, oceans---

Giving is a gift of free will.

We can give of our time, energy,
compassion, patience and understanding.

The more we give, the more it grows.

The matrix teaches scarcity--
by holding back--
what is rightly for all.

Lets give freely---
Break the program---
Change the language of your thoughts;
and your actions will speak freely---

Giving, Loving and Allowing

I Love You
I'm sorry
Please forgive me
Thank-you
     Ho'oponopono

Not My Kuleana*
by Cheryl

Divine Neutrality.
Someone asked me about this---

Recently,
I had an experience--
talking to someone,
who in return
gave me
a look of disdain---

I knew it was not my fault
nor my problem
if anyone
does or does not
appreciate me.

That is them
and
their stuff.

I remind myself,
that I'm worthy,
and beautiful.

A famous quote goes--
"We are born to make manifest the glory of God that is within us...as we let our light shine, we unconsciously give others permission to do the same" Marrianne Williamson

As we are liberated from our own fear,
our presence
automatically liberates others.

*Kuleana, Hawaiian for responsibility.

> "The soul looketh steadily forwards,
> Erecting a world before her,
> Leaving worlds behind her."
> Ralph Waldo Emerson

Birth of Light, A Sister and Brother Poem
by Rita Chambers and John Raifsnider(Italics)
Jan. 23, 2023 after the passing of Rita's lifemate Ed.

Sister,
I see you shining out!
What burns within you is too great a sun to be contained.

Our Spirits are free.
Our hearts are on fire!

This long song to guide our stride.
It takes time to place a new rhythm in our step.

They cannot harvest my Soul.
They cannot take my Desire!*

Dear,
What new Music longs through us
to Sing out?

We are part of the Earth, part of the sky.
The song of light does not end when we die.

We were born into darkness.
Every step onward, a birth of Light!

Our Spirits are free.
Our Hearts are on fire!

We shall seek and we shall find what draws us out,
just as your hand draws out from your Heart.

Yes, my Brother,
They cannot harvest my Soul.
They cannot take my Desire!

*Origins of Desire, Latin "Sidar" or "DeSidare".
Historically understood as: "From the Stars" or "Heavenly Body".

In the Shadows We Met
by Jennifer H.

In the shadows we met,
I wanted to play
not knowing
what it meant to stay.

Your fire burned darkly
consuming my essence,
whenever I was in your presence

Entangled and entwined
as we danced
this wicked dance---
the push and pull
of want and need,
self-hatred and greed.

In the shadows we met,
our darkest parts
Excited
to tear each other apart--
the intense feeling
of lust and need
driving you to feed--

My soul your meal
keeping you
from having to feel.

With your pain in my heart
I didn't know where to start
so I let it flow--
not wanting
to let go,

Sinking deeper within
your enchanting
dark desires
feeding my own twisted fire--
awakening the demon within
wanting you under my skin--

Until
I got stretched
too thin--
I had let
too much of *you* in.

My own parts
Lost
in darkness--
with your shadow
wrapped
around my heart.

I realized
that we have to part--
you will no longer feed
off my essence.

I will never dim in your presence.
My etheric celestial fire
Intensely burning
keeps me from turning.

In the shadows we met.

Now,
I dance with light in my heart,
knowing how to keep the shadows at bay--
No longer willing to play.

I hope one day
you'll find your way.

Many thanks to these contributors:

Christine O'Brien

Maria Lodes

A'Marie B. Thomas-Brown

Rajni Lerman

Cody Ray Richardson

Susan Grace

Sam Garrett

Mercy Talley

Dave Harvey

Uncle Chester

Eileen Casey

Steve Keating

Rita Chambers

John Raifsnider

Jennifer H.

and the unknown author

Author page--

Cheryl Lunar Wind lives in the Mount Shasta area in a little town called Weed. She is a practicer of Mayan cosmology, Lakota ceremony, Star Knowledge and the Universal Laws including the Law of One. Her hobbies are writing poetry, music, dance, drum circles and love for all life; plant, animal and crystal. Cheryl has been a guide and spiritual teacher for many years. Now she shares wisdom and wit through poetry, and has published poetry books; Know Your Way, We Are One, Follow the White Rabbit, Love Your Light, LIFE: Shared thru Poetry, Come to Mount Shasta: Sacred Path Poetry, We Are Light and co-authored We Are Forever: Awaken With Poetry.

Testimonials---

"Cheryl's poetry is very inspiring--particularly the way she compares life with the forces of nature. There is a special element in her poems that opens my heart and fills my soul with divine possibilities."
Giovanna Taormina, Co-Founder, One Circle Foundation

"Cheryl's poems have helped me to uncover and honor my own hidden memories. The beauty of her spirit is evident in each tender, insightful passage."
Marguerite Lorimer, www.earthalive.com

"A rare collection filled with raw, courageous honesty. Thought provoking words that will stop you in your tracks."
Snow Thorner, ED Open Sky Gallery, Montague, California

"When wisdom, guidance, confirming comfort, ect. arrives to us humans--from beings with the perspective of other realms--it is a divine gift. Especially in the form of what we call poetry, and through a being with no agenda; Cheryl Lunar Wind simply shares what source gives her!"
--Dragon Love (Thomas) Budde